Our La Salette Mission:

To Reconcile Her People With Her Son

by Fr. Normand Theroux, M.S.

Missionaries of La Salette Corporation
915 Maple Avenue
Hartford, CT 06114-2330, USA

web site: www.lasalette.org

Imprimi Potest:

Very Rev. Fr. Rene Butler, M.S., Provincial
Superior, Missionaries of Our Lady of La
Salette, Province of Mary, Mother of the
Americas, 915 Maple Avenue, Hartford,
CT 06114-2330 USA

Printed in the United States of America

Booklet Design and Digital Formatting: Jack Battersby and Fr. Ron
Gagne, M.S.

This and other La Salette titles available in E-book format at www.
lasalette.org

ISBN: 978-1-946956-15-6

Introduction

We know well some beliefs that are central to our Catholic life and ministry: life in Christ; the Trinity; belief and trust in a personal God and Savior; the prominent place of prayer; faith, hope and love; and, lastly, concern for the neighbor and for ourselves.

We see the qualities for today's La Salette reconcilers as building upon or deepening those Catholic qualities we learned early in life. We speak of these as special because we can notice how Our Lady highlighted, expressed or modeled them during her discourse at La Salette.

Furthermore, Our Lady never intended to be comprehensive in her message: she never mentioned the Incarnation, the Resurrection, Pentecost or the Trinity for example, which are the pillars of our faith. She gave a specific message on specific topics for specific reasons.

The Beautiful Lady's discourse included qualities not meant only for those already connected to La Salette because she told the two children to "make this known to all my people." Indeed, her words are a summons, a mandate for the entire world. Her message is rooted in St. Paul's own call to be reconcilers (2 Corinthians 5:17-20;6:1).

Fr. Normand Theroux, M.S.

From The Editor:

This collection of reflections on La Salette, originally titled, "The Caring Community", was first published privately for the La Salette Province of the Immaculate Heart of Mary, in preparation for their Province Chapter.

These reflections have been reconfigured, expanded, and now published as a series of reflections on "Our La Salette Mission".

I

The event of La Salette is a biblically-centered Apparition of Mary which happened on September 19, 1846. Fr. Theroux's comments as a scripture scholar and long-time La Salette Missionary apply the age-old La Salette message to our daily living.

The structure of these materials includes: 1) a Scripture passage, 2) a Reflection, 3) Reflection questions. 4) a Prayer on the theme, and concludes with 5) the praying of the La Salette Invocation. We have arranged these reflections and written new content for numbers 3 & 4 above.

This resource is designed to be used by individuals or groups in their reflection on God's Word and the La Salette message for anyone interested in or connected to the Apparition of Our Lady of La Salette.

Fr. Ron Gagne, M.S.
Sept. 19, 2017, Attleboro, MA, USA

Contents

1

Mary's Wish To Reconcile Her People With Her Son

Scripture: 2 Corinthians 5:17-20;6:1 (*The Ministry Of Reconciliation*)

So whoever is in Christ is a new creation: the old things have passed away; behold, new things have come. And all this is from God, who has reconciled us to himself through Christ and given us the ministry of reconciliation, namely, God was reconciling the world to himself in Christ, not counting their trespasses against them and entrusting to us the message of reconciliation. So we are ambassadors for Christ, as if God were appealing through us. We implore you on behalf of Christ, be reconciled to God... Working together, then, we appeal to you not to receive the grace of God in vain.

Reflection:

Reconciliation is change. What usually comes to mind when we hear the word reconciliation is that two people, or two parties, who had once been friends and have become alienated, have now renewed their former relationship and are friends once more.

St. Paul goes to the root of that renewal event and uses a word for

1

reconciliation which means essentially "to change." Before the friends can come together again something has to happen within them to bring reconciliation about. In human relationships this can happen through talking and listening, through explanations of past actions as well as through seeking forgiveness from the injured party.

At La Salette, the Lady clearly had change in mind. The great news is that her people has to submit in order to be reconciled with God. This kind of reconciliation is a gift that can only come from him. The initiative is his, this is why she speaks in her Son's name. But as often happens between true friends who have quarreled and have renewed their friendship, the new relationship will deepen, become more intimate. This is the promise of La Salette.

Reflection Questions:

- When in your life have you had to change anything of importance?
- What event or situation unexpectedly changed the life of someone you know?

Prayer:

Mary, Mother of Reconciliation, your appearance at La Salette was another example of God's care for us through your loving presence.

You came to share the message of your Son and renew his call to change our lives, become a new creation, and, in Paul's words, live as true ambassadors of reconciliation.

Open our hearts to your message and change us into a better likeness of your Son, who lives with the Father and the Holy Spirit, one God, for ever and ever. **Amen.**

Invocation:
Our Lady of La Salette, Reconciler of Sinners, pray without ceasing for us who have recourse to you.

2

Mary Shares Her Words And Her Tears

Scripture: Isaiah 53:2-5 (*The Suffering Servant*)

He grew up like a sapling before him, like a shoot from the parched earth; He had no majestic bearing to catch our eye, no beauty to draw us to him. He was spurned and avoided by men, a man of suffering, knowing pain, Like one from whom you turn your face, spurned, and we held him in no esteem. Yet it was our pain that he bore, our sufferings he endured. We thought of him as stricken, struck down by God and afflicted, But he was pierced for our sins, crushed for our iniquity. He bore the punishment that makes us whole, by his wounds we were healed...

Reflection:

No one can say that La Salette is a colorless, cold apparition. Our Lady did not appear on this high mountain to hand down a few warnings and prescribe prayers and practices. Nothing calm and cold about this event. The children, Maximin and Mélanie, saw her sitting on a stone, her face in her hands, and she was weeping.

3

Tears are always an overflow. They are pressured out of the heart by an excess of pain or joy. This is a case of pure pain.

Tears are not a merely physiological reality. They are also, as is the case here, signs of loving concern. Christ wept over Jerusalem because he was concerned. People weep because they care. Tears are the opposite of fish-coldness, indifference, disinterest and apathy. They signal involvement and the intense will to be part of another person's life.

These tears are La Salette's most powerful unspoken message. The beautiful Lady weeps but she never refers to her tears, never so much as alludes to them. They are meant to speak for themselves and they do. They are an unspoken message but they add a crucial dimension to her words.

When we read the message of La Salette, we must remember that it was spoken by someone in tears. Without the tears, the 'a capella' words would take on an icy aloofness, even a kind of muffled ferocity. The words she spoke had to be spoken. The Lady's 'problem' was how to communicate this sad news without sowing worldwide panic and the threat of Armageddon by famine instead of fire...

The Lady's sign of affection, the universally accepted sign of a mother's desperate love has always been tears. At La Salette, they are liquid sorrow, molten streams of pain running down the Lady's face and a very obvious show of love. Whoever reads the message or speaks about it must remember to place the tough message in the context of the care and affection made evident by the Lady's persistent weeping. Maximin and Mélanie never forgot to say that the Lady wept all the while she spoke. The "tears flowed and flowed" they said.

The tears should be remembered for another reason. They highlight the words and give urgency and crucial importance to the entire message. If someone from heaven, and the Blessed Virgin at that, is provoked to tears over disrespect for the Day of the Lord and the Name of Jesus, then the word is out that these offenses are more evil than people think they are and should be carefully avoided.

And then, there is the following point: if the words she speaks are a message from her Son, then why wouldn't the tears themselves communicate something from the very Person of Christ. If her words reflect his will, then why shouldn't the tears mirror God's own care and affection? The Woman speaks the words of Christ. Why wouldn't she weep the tears of God?

Reflection Questions:

- When have the tears of another touched your heart?
- How are Mary's tears at La Salette, in some way, the tears of God?

Prayer:

Mary, Our Weeping Mother of La Salette, your painful experience of the passion and death of your Son has brought many of us to tears.

You are truly a shining example of a Mother's unending love for her child. The image of your strong faith and faithful endurance encourage us as we bear the challenges of this life.

Ask your Son to lift us up by the grace of his resurrection as we continue to live our Christian life with faith and hope in your Son, who lives with the Father and the Holy Spirit, one God, for ever and ever. **Amen.**

Invocation:

Our Lady of La Salette, Reconciler of Sinners, pray without ceasing for us who have recourse to you.

3

Mary Warns Of A Great Famine

Scripture: Amos 4:6-9 (*God Warns His People*)

Though I made your teeth clean of food in all your cities, and made bread scarce in all your dwellings, Yet you did not return to me…And I withheld the rain from you when the harvest was still three months away; I sent rain upon one city but not upon another; One field was watered by rain, but the one I did not water dried up; Two or three cities staggered to another to drink water but were not satisfied; Yet you did not return to me… I struck you with blight and mildew; locusts devoured your gardens and vineyards, the caterpillar consumed your fig trees and olive trees; Yet you did not return to me…

Reflection:

Our faith is made of mysteries. An apparition may not be a mystery but it is a symbol and a reminder of mystery. The globe of light surrounding Mary, the Cross with its hammer and pincers, her message with her warnings and promises – all these unusual signs harken back to the mystery of God's relationship with us, his people…

Our ordinary daily lives also have their mysteries – the well-being of evil, the misery of the poor, the suffering of innocent children, the violation of women, and those people who lose their faith in God. All of these are a mystery… Yet just as God is part of our lives, so mystery is an enduring part of it as well. We live by what we sometimes cannot fathom or understand.

As Fr. Gerard La Roche, M.S, wrote:

"(With the concerned voice of a prophet, Mary warns her children to return to her Son): *'If my people will not submit, I shall be forced to let go the arm of my Son. It is so strong and so heavy that I can no longer withhold it.'* And there follows the tender recalling of Mary's own efforts on behalf of the offenders who are also her children: *'How long a time do I suffer for you. If I would not have my Son abandon you, I am compelled to pray to him without ceasing.'* She adds, *'A great famine is coming. Before the famine comes, children under seven will be seized with trembling and die in the arms of those who hold them. The rest will do penance through the famine.'*"

The deepest mystery manifested at La Salette is the expression of God's love for humankind. How and why was this done? It was done by the way God spoke, and still speaks to us. Since the love of God cannot ever be understood in human terms, so it is expressed, as at La Salette, for example, in terms that perhaps don't make sense to us humans, in words and ideas that we human beings sometimes cannot fathom.

Just as the loving promise of "self-sown potatoes" doesn't make sense to us, so also the love of God is so great that it often makes no sense to us. And just as the impossibility of "stones becoming mounds of wheat" makes little sense to us, it is in the same way that God loves us, with that same lack of sense that we may not initially understand or appreciate.

We note also that these figures of speech are spoken for our benefit, our own happiness and encouragement, in the sense that they are, at the outset, concerned with food for nourishment and fulfillment but more deeply symbolize that better days are coming for God's people.

Reflection Questions:

- Do you remember an example of being warned as a youngster by your parents about something important (or you warning your own child about something)?
- In the scripture passage from the book of Amos, what feelings or impressions do you get from Amos's recounting of God's repeated warnings to God's own people?

Prayer:

Mary, Queen of prophets, your words of warning were a stark reminder that we have strayed too often from the message and ways and of your Son.

Your words at La Salette echo those of the Father with his people Israel, and those of your own Son to his wayward people. May your merciful concern for your people soon be understood and bear fruit.

Help us realize where we need to repent and how we can open ourselves the enduring grace of God's mercy and forgiveness. We ask this through your Son, who lives with the Father and the Holy Spirit, one God, for ever and ever. **Amen.**

Invocation:

Our Lady of La Salette, Reconciler of Sinners, pray without ceasing for us who have recourse to you.

4

Mary Invites Us To
"Come Near" And "Be Not Afraid"

Scripture: Luke 1:26-33 (*The Annunciation Of Mary By An Angel*)

In the sixth month, the angel Gabriel was sent from God to a town of Galilee called Nazareth, to a virgin betrothed to a man named Joseph, of the house of David, and the virgin's name was Mary. And coming to her, he said, "Hail, favored one! The Lord is with you." But she was greatly troubled at what was said and pondered what sort of greeting this might be. Then the angel said to her, "Do not be afraid, Mary, for you have found favor with God. Behold, you will conceive in your womb and bear a son, and you shall name him Jesus. He will be great and will be called Son of the Most High, and the Lord God will give him the throne ofDavid his father, and he will rule over the house of Jacob forever, and of his kingdom there will be no end."

Reflection:

At La Salette, the Beautiful Lady began her message by reassuring the children: *"Come near, my children, do not be afraid. I am here to tell you great news."* She succeeded marvelously well in dispelling their

9

fear. They later said that their fear left them immediately.

They drew so close to her that no one could have walked between them and the Lady. What might have been a frightening experience became a moment in life they would look upon as the most beautiful half-hour of their existence. They ran after her and would have asked her to take them with her if they had known she was "a great saint." The Lady became "their Lady" that day and remained so to the end of their lives.

She also told the children: *"I am here to tell you great news."* It is interesting to note that in scripture, each time God enjoins his people or an individual not to fear, the ensuing message or action is always related to salvation or reconciliation. Can it be that many of our difficulties in dealing with or relating with God originate with fear and foreboding? To be reconciled means to have changed from a life of fear to a life of respect and love.

Reflection Questions:

- When have you (or a friend) received exceedingly good news?
- Can you identify with Maximin and Melanie as they were surprised and initially fearful of the globe of light in the upper pasture on that September day so long ago?

Prayer:

Mary, Comforter of the Fearful, you yourself experienced the fearful moment when the angel greeted you with an invitation to become the Mother of God. By God's grace your accepted this precious call.

As you first appeared at La Salette to these two unsuspecting children, your glorious presence surprised and upset them. Yet your loving concern and invitation to "come near" melted their fear and drew them to draw closer to your tearful face.

Help us always to draw closer to your Son without fear or hesitation, like Maximin and Melanie, and hear his message in your words of welcome, faith and hope. We ask this through your Son, who lives with the Father and the Holy Spirit, one God, for ever and ever. Amen.

Invocation:

Our Lady of La Salette, Reconciler of Sinners, pray without ceasing for us who have recourse to you.

5

Mary wants us to Listen to her Message

Scripture: Isaiah 55:3,6-11 (*Pay Attention And Come To Me*)

Pay attention and come to me; listen, that you may have life. I will make with you an everlasting covenant, the steadfast loyalty promised to David... Seek the Lord while he may be found, call upon him while he is near. Let the wicked forsake their way, and sinners their thoughts; Let them turn to the Lord to find mercy; to our God, who is generous in forgiving.

For my thoughts are not your thoughts, nor are your ways my ways – oracle of the Lord. For as the heavens are higher than the earth, so are my ways higher than your ways, my thoughts higher than your thoughts. Yet just as from the heavens the rain and snow come down And do not return there till they have watered the earth, making it fertile and fruitful, Giving seed to the one who sows and bread to the one who eats, So shall my word be that goes forth from my mouth; It shall not return to me empty, but shall do what pleases me, achieving the end for which I sent it.

Reflection:

At La Salette, Our Lady highlights her Son's reactions to our sins.

The most offensive one is that of refusing to accomplish God's will in our lives. It is followed immediately in the discourse by the most ominous threat; namely, the risk of being set aside by her Son. *"If my Son is not to abandon you, I am obliged to pray to him without ceasing,"* she says.

It is almost unthinkable that Christ, who is the Way, should abandon someone in mid-journey. We know in fact that this is a figure of speech, that God never abandons or casts anyone off. We are the ones who do the abandoning and the setting aside. And God, who is the God of freedom, will not force the issue. But there is real suffering in heaven for those who have left Christ who is the Way, the Truth and the Life.

The Beautiful Lady said that her people paid *"no attention"* to her constant suffering as she holds back the arm of her Son. She also reproached her people for not seeing the signs of the times when the potatoes rotted. *"You paid no least heed,"* she said. These two oversights are the two most overlooked statements in the message of La Salette.

The sins she underscored were not the crass acts that make headlines. Not honoring God in his Name and on his day, not worshiping, not praying are the root causes, the deep-seated sins against God that bring on those "sins against the neighbor." The Lady says, without actually pronouncing the words, that serving God and serving the neighbor are not two acts, but one.

On the face of it, the La Salette message is limited in its demands: Mass, prayer, penance, and respect for Christ's name appear to be the bare bones of religion, that minimum without which all ties with God cease to exist. On the other hand, when these elements are observed well, they launch an intimate and powerful Christian life, for all of Christian life is based on those demands.

Reflection Questions:

- Are there family or friends to whom you have paid little attention? Why?
- Give some instances of where and when you have gone out of your way to serve God or your neighbor.

Prayer:

Mary, Attentive Mother of us all, your constant concern for the happiness and welfare of your children shown so well through your merciful apparition at La Salette speak volumes.

Your motherly interest in the spiritual welfare of each of your children is truly astonishing. And, above all, your ceaseless efforts to protect and inspire your children is without measure.

With all the attention, we are asked to give to the ordinary concerns of daily living, help us each day to faithfully serve both God and neighbor, as Jesus has requested of us. We ask this through your Son, who lives with the Father and the Holy Spirit, one God, for ever and ever. **Amen.**

Invocation:

Our Lady of La Salette, Reconciler of Sinners, pray without ceasing for us who have recourse to you.

6

Mary's Warnings And Concern For Our Salvation

Scripture: John 14: 1-2,7a,8-9,10b,11 (*Jesus Encourages His Disciples*)

"Do not let your hearts be troubled. You have faith in God; have faith also in me. In my Father's house there are many dwelling places. If there were not, would I have told you that I am going to prepare a place for you?... If you know me, then you will also know my Father... Philip said to him, "Master, show us the Father, and that will be enough for us." Jesus said to him, "Have I been with you for so long a time and you still do not know me, Philip? Whoever has seen me has seen the Father... The words that I speak to you I do not speak on my own. The Father who dwells in me is doing his works...

Reflection:

There is no doubt that Our Lady of La Salette referred to the existence of social sin. The individual, personal sins existed in 1846 also, because each cart-driver who used the name of her Son, each person who worked on Sunday and did not go to Mass, offended God personally. Why then should God punish society for the sins of individuals? The reasons involve the influence of the

individual's conduct, good or bad, on the community as a whole.

We might suggest that in cases such as those mentioned at La Salette (missing Mass and/or working on Sunday, using the name of Christ in vain, avoiding penance), the practices had become so widespread that individual correction would prove futile. The evil had become endemic. All her people had been affected by it. It had also been long lasting.

The punishment was not to be meted out because of a few brief incursions into evil. The Lady said: *"How long a time I have suffered for you! If my Son is not to abandon you, I am obliged to plead with him without ceasing."*

To counter the evil mounting to heaven like an obscene cloud, the Lady had to resort to constant, unrelenting entreaty before God. As the Lady speaks, one senses a sorrow beyond that of tears. There is a deep-seated grief at having to punish, to inflict pain upon her people. First, the entire threat of punishment is made conditional. *"If my people refuse to submit... If I want my Son not to abandon you..."*

Then, reasons for the coming punishment are amply provided. The people must be made to see that the punishment fits the crime. The violation of the law of Sunday rest, blasphemy, omission of Mass, absence of penance are injustices to God. Yet one cannot avoid noting how hesitantly God punishes... when it has come to that.

Reflection Questions:

• Can you identify with Christ's concern about the lack of understanding of his own disciples? Have you had similar concern for anyone in your family or friends?
• In what ways did Mary express her concern for the two children standing before her?

Prayer:

Mary, Loving Mother, your disappointment with us, your children, and our unchristian way of life has caused you much grief. You came to La Salette not only to chide your wayward children but also to express your concern for us and indicate a way back to your Son.

Your expressions at La Salette of concern for our daily lives stir our hearts and prompt us to reflect on our personal situation of faith.

Continue to inspire us to open our lives to the grace of your Son who wishes all of his children to come to him and make our home with him. We ask this through your Son, who lives with the Father and the Holy Spirit, one God, for ever and ever. **Amen.**

Invocation:

Our Lady of La Salette, Reconciler of Sinners, pray without ceasing for us who have recourse to you.

7

Mary's Promises

Scripture: Isaiah 41:8a,9-10,13,19 (*The Wasteland Shall Bloom*)

But you, Israel, my servant, ...You whom I have taken from the ends of the earth and summoned from its far-off places, To whom I have said, You are my servant; I chose you, I have not rejected you – Do not fear: I am with you; do not be anxious: I am your God.

I will strengthen you, I will help you, I will uphold you with my victorious right hand. For I am the Lord, your God, who grasp your right hand; It is I who say to you, Do not fear, I will help you. I will open up rivers on the bare heights, and fountains in the broad valleys; I will turn the wilderness into a marshland, and the dry ground into springs of water. In the wilderness I will plant the cedar, acacia, myrtle, and olive; In the wasteland I will set the cypress, together with the plane tree and the pine, That all may see and know, observe and understand, That the hand of the Lord has done this, the Holy One of Israel has created it.

Reflection:

At La Salette, the great moment of promise came when the Lady said: *"If my people are converted, the rocks will become piles of wheat and it will be found that the potatoes have sown themselves."* The promise is purposely exaggerated to give free expression to the joy in heaven over the return of even one sinner. And yet, the exaggeration is only apparent since the joy of God and the gift of grace are events far more delightful than a miraculous harvest. Like the prophets, the Lady uses an image people will understand to express a joy that no one on earth can fathom.

At La Salette the Lady's promises are of Messianic extravagance. If her people obey the will of her Son, stones will become mounds of wheat and potatoes will grow as if self-sown. These two signs of bounty could, of course, only be produced by the Lord himself, although they never actually occurred. But exaggerated as they seem, they are symbols of gifts greater than any miracle mounds of wheat and self-sown potatoes.

The gifts of God are always a sign of God himself. His presence in his gifts is always his greatest gift. Bumper crops of wheat and potatoes are the divine rhetoric of love and joy that are as incredible and as "impossible" as stones becoming wheat and potatoes self-sowing in the land.

Reflection Questions:

- When has God surprised you with an unexpected abundance or occurrence, echoing Isaiah's words: God promises that springs of water will miraculously arise from dry, barren land?
- Mary has tried to encourage us to listen to her Son. When have you encouraged another person to persevere in some challenge or hardship for the love of God?

Prayer:

Mary, Mother of God's People, we, your children, gather before you, asking that you continue to intercede for us as you have promised.

We need your words of hope to lift us up so that we can count on the grace of your Son and your unceasing prayers in our daily struggles to persist in our faith and trust in our loving God.

As we await the second coming of your Son, give us the vision of hope that only you and your Son can give us. We ask this through your Son, who lives with the Father and the Holy Spirit, one God, for ever and ever. **Amen.**

Invocation:

Our Lady of La Salette, Reconciler of Sinners, pray without ceasing for us who have recourse to you.

8

Mary's Appreciation For The Mass And Other Habits Of Faith

Scripture: 1 Corinthians 11:23-26 (*The earliest written account of the Last Supper*)

For I received from the Lord what I also handed on to you, that the Lord Jesus, on the night he was handed over, took bread, and, after he had given thanks, broke it and said, "This is my body that is for you. Do this in remembrance of me." In the same way also the cup, after supper, saying, "This cup is the new covenant in my blood. Do this, as often as you drink it, in remembrance of me." For as often as you eat this bread and drink the cup, you proclaim the death of the Lord until he comes.

Reflection:

The Mass is the Easter Mystery lived in everyday life. It is Christ's own self-giving. In the Eucharist we are to acquire what we pray for and be what we perform. If we become that, then we will become what the La Salette mystery requires us to be; namely, what Christ in the Eucharist actually is.

The Lady's message is strong on the matter of the Eucharist: *"Only a few rather old women go to Mass in the summer. Everyone else works every Sunday all summer long. And in winter, when they don't know what to do with themselves, they go to Mass only to scoff at religion."* A reconciling person is one with a very special devotion to the Eucharist, because the first goal of the Eucharist is Redemption, which includes recon-

ciliation with her Son.

The Beautiful Lady is our role-model disciple. She is the apostle-disciple mandated by the Lord to bear his message. Her first words, *"I am here to tell you great news"*, implies a sending, a mission. There is no doubt that she has come in her Son's name and to accomplish his will. In fact, her Son is directly referred to six times throughout the message.

Her message centers on him: her people abuse his name, violate the holiness of his day and scoff at the Mass. Her assigned duties are to intercede with him, to hold back his arm. *"I am obliged to entreat him without ceasing,"* she says. Nothing and no one else is remotely alluded to or hinted at during the apparition except offenses against him and the rewards he will bestow if his people obey.

It can also be noted that the sins mentioned in the apparition at La Salette are all personal sins against the Lord himself. These are the faults that silently undermine the respect a friend owes to a friend and erode the ties of intimacy and trust that are the very soil of love. No discipleship can prosper or exist in their company

Reflection Questions:

- Do you remember any part of the day of your First Communion?
- Have you ever encouraged or invited anyone to come to Mass with you?

Prayer:

Mary, First Disciple of Jesus, your life of love and willing service are so consistent from the very first words of the angel inviting you to be the mother of the Savior.

Our Blessed Lady, in whom the Lord himself made his dwelling, is referred to as the Ark of the New Covenant, the place where the glory of the Lord dwells. She is the dwelling of God with humanity.

Her words at La Salette support the importance of Eucharist and urge us to hold closely this true gift from God that is our weekly celebration of the Lord's Supper. May we always keep alive in our hearts this important belief of our Catholic faith. We ask this through your Son, who lives with the Father and the Holy Spirit, one God, for ever and ever. **Amen.**

Invocation:

Our Lady of La Salette, Reconciler of Sinners, pray without ceasing for us who have recourse to you.

9

Mary Gives Us A Mission

Scripture: Matthew 28:16-20 (*The Commissioning of the Disciples*)

The eleven disciples went to Galilee, to the mountain to which Jesus had ordered them. When they saw him, they worshiped, but they doubted. Then Jesus approached and said to them, "All power in heaven and on earth has been given to me. Go, therefore, and make disciples of all nations, baptizing them in the name of the Father, and of the Son, and of the holy Spirit, teaching them to observe all that I have commanded you. And behold, I am with you always, until the end of the age."

Reflection:

At La Salette we are reminded of another priority of our gospel mission; namely to *"...make this known to all my people."* The children were sent out on what was for them a seemingly impossible mission. They were too young. They were illiterate. They were in no way religious; in fact, they did not even realize that the Lady speaking to them was the Blessed Virgin.

If the truth be told, these two children were not especially lovable: Maximin was a scatterbrain; Melanie was constantly uncommunicative and morose. Neither of them knew the language of the country they were to "evangelize". According to any human standard of competence, they were eminently unsuited for the mission that was assigned to them. Further, as they themselves later realized, their entire lives were changed forever. Maximin said that he would have been content to live out his life in the quiet of his mountains instead of trying to "live up" to the immensely stressful demands of his new mission.

They Lady selected them very much in the manner in which her Son had chosen his disciples. She clearly did not choose people who, according to popular wisdom, were qualified for the mission they were to fulfill. In fact, one might say that the choice of the children as unqualified was made abundantly obvious, almost in an exaggerated manner.

This mission, the Lady seemed to say by implication, would be accomplished by children who would need the constant presence of a special grace. The simple fact that these "ambassadors" were mere children, chosen on purpose, is a manifestly divine "code" to say that this mission would be fulfilled by the Lord's constant love and presence. The children were messengers but they soon became a living proof of the heavenly origin of the "great news" they were spreading.

The message they would communicate to the world was a "life" message. These children were not chosen in church or in school, or during Mass or prayer. They were selected while at work, just as the Lord chose his own disciples by the lakeside while they were fishing or cleansing their nets. The Lady specifically wanted them – these children and no other. And so she went to the mountain and appeared to them while they were looking for their cows, in the rush of their work.

Reflection Questions:

- When have you felt unprepared from some task or vocation?
- Whom have you seen blossom into a stronger, more capable person?

Prayer:

Mary, Queen of Apostles, hear our prayer as we lift up our eyes to you, our help and our shield. Guide us in the path of your Son, who is the Way, the Truth, and the Life.

In your heavenly visit at La Salette, you, like your Son, gave us a mandate, reminding everyone that they are to be disciples to all nations, far beyond the confines of the Holy Mountain of La Salette.

Keep us focused on our mission of reconciliation, faithfully announcing to everyone your message – ultimately the words and mission of your Son. Give us the faith, wisdom and courage necessary to complete our mandate before we meet God face to face in the heavenly kingdom. We ask this through your Son, who lives with the Father and the Holy Spirit, one God, for ever and ever. **Amen.**

Invocation:

Our Lady of La Salette, Reconciler of Sinners, pray without ceasing for us who have recourse to you.

10

Mary Loves And
Respects Her People

Scripture: Exodus 6:7;19:5-6; 20:2a; 29:45-46 (*You Are My People*)

I will take you as my own people, and I will be your God; and you
will know that I, the Lord, am your God who has freed you from the
burdens of the Egyptians... Now, if you obey me completely and keep
my covenant, you will be my treasured possession among all peoples,
though all the earth is mine. You will be to me a kingdom of priests, a
holy nation... I am the Lord your God, who brought you out of the
land of Egypt, out of the house of slavery... I will dwell in the midst
of the Israelites and will be their God. They shall know that I, the
Lord, am their God who brought them out of the land of Egypt, so
that I, the Lord, their God, might dwell among them.

Reflection:

Everything Our Lady speaks about at La Salette has reference to *"my people"*. The Mass, famine, prayer, penance, her suffering, the harvests, rotting wheat, spoiling walnuts, going to the butcher shop "like dogs", working on Sunday, the farm of Coin – all of these referred to people. Her reason for appearing are people: *"Come near, my children. I have come to give you great news. If my people will not submit, I am forced to let go of the arm of my Son."*

We might also insist on respect for people. One has to admire the Lady's wondrous respect for the two little urchins standing before her. If they had been royalty, they would not have received more consideration. She speaks to them politely. She speaks in their own patois when she learns that they do not understand French. She does not ask of them that which they cannot give: she ask that they say only one "Our Father" and one "Hail Mary", nothing more.

She gives Maximin a practical example of rotting wheat, an instance taken from his own life. Her words betray only a hint of the deep respect she has towards them. She also shows them, by her tone of voice, by her general attitude, that she loved them.

The children were deeply saddened when the Lady left them and disappeared into the horizon. "If we had known she was a great saint," they said, "we would have asked her to take us with her." The Lady had expressed this love and inspired this requital of affection only after one half-hour in their presence. This is the kind of sovereign respect for the human person that is needed in our common ministry of reconciliation.

Reflection Questions:

- What are one thing you learn about the relationship between God and God's people in this passage from the book of Exodus?
- What is one quality in Mary's apparition at La Salette that you see reflected in her Son?

Prayer:

Mary, Mother of the needy, you welcome us as God welcomed his own people into the safety of his presence, following the light of God's guidance.

In your words at La Salette, you respect our needs and ask us to keep your Son at the center of our daily life. Your gentle reminders of our need for daily prayer, respect for your Son's name, and using the habits of Lent to draw us closer to him and his life.

Assist us in our daily journey to follow your Son as his beloved people. Help us, in turn, to welcome others back to the ways and message of Jesus. We ask this through your Son, who lives with the Father and the Holy Spirit, one God, for ever and ever. **Amen.**

Invocation:

Our Lady of La Salette, Reconciler of Sinners, pray without ceasing for us who have recourse to you.

11

Mary Brings A Message Of Compassion

Scripture: Matthew 9:35-38 (*The Compassion of Jesus*)

Jesus went around to all the towns and villages, teaching in their synagogues, proclaiming the gospel of the kingdom, and curing every disease and illness. At the sight of the crowds, his heart was moved with pity for them because they were troubled and abandoned, like sheep without a shepherd. Then he said to his disciples, "The harvest is abundant but the laborers are few; so ask the master of the harvest to send out laborers for his harvest."

Reflection:

One day, Maximin's father had suffered enough of his drinking friends' taunts and ridicule over his son's vision of the Beautiful Lady. He forbade the boy to speak about it any longer. Maximin replied: "But, father, the Lady spoke about you too." Taken aback, the "Charron (wheelmaker) Giraud" listened in awe as Maximin told him about the incident of the "Terre du Coin" (a field at a four corners). It was easier to believe that Mémin – Maximin's nickname – could be a court page than to think he could remember such a trifling incident.

Mr. Giraud was astounded that the Lady should have noticed and remembered such a meaningless scene, that she should have heard his own words in conversation with the owner of the farm as well as with his son. There was simply no one else in sight in the fields that day. Touched to his very soul, Mr. Giraud allowed Maximin to spread his "good news". God had indeed shown that his love and care are constant.

Mary's apparition contains many other signs of God's kindness and affection for us. Her tears are the most obvious sign of God's care and concern in modern times.

Reflection Questions:

- When have you reached out in compassion to the needs of another?
- In being confronted with the deep needs of another person, when have you hesitated or even decided not to help them – even for some good reason?

Prayer:

Mary, Mother of Compassion, your Son's example of pity for his troubled people is mirrored in your words and actions at La Salette.

Your thoughtful mention of the Maximin's father's fear of not being able to provide food for his family touched your heart and urged you to remind Maximin of the sad event at the field of Coin.

Continue to touch and change our hearts that we, in turn, may reach out in compassion to those who need to feel the concern your Son has for them and their loved ones. We ask this through your Son, who lives with the Father and the Holy Spirit, one God, for ever and ever. **Amen.**

Invocation:

Our Lady of La Salette, Reconciler of Sinners, pray without ceasing for us who have recourse to you.

12

Mary Adapts To Her People

Scripture: Philippians 2:5-11 (*Jesus Emptied Himself for Love of Us*)

Have among yourselves the same attitude that is also yours in Christ Jesus, Who, though he was in the form of God, did not regard equality with God something to be grasped. Rather, he emptied himself, taking the form of a slave, coming in human likeness; and found human in appearance, he humbled himself, becoming obedient to death, even death on a cross.

Because of this, God greatly exalted him and bestowed on him the name that is above every name, that at the name of Jesus every knee should bend, of those in heaven and on earth and under the earth, and every tongue confess that Jesus Christ is Lord, to the glory of God the Father.

Reflection:

At La Salette, the Lady chose two cailloux – or little "pebbles from the road" as the French writer, Léon Bloy, called them – from a village existing on the edge of misery. Mother-like, she asked them if they said their prayers and was understanding enough and knew them enough to prescribe a minimum of one *Our Father* and one *Hail Mary* morning and evening. She manifested interest in the local crops as well as in local people. She was interested and knowledge-able enough to mention potatoes and raisins and walnuts and wheat. Her concern was sharp and individual enough to see two men and a boy walking through a field and sadly watching wheat turn to dust in their hands.

She was attentive enough to people to hear Maximin's father say to his son: "Well, my son, eat some bread this year, anyhow. I don't know who will be eating any next year if the wheat continues to spoil like that." Even Maximin had completely forgotten the incident and had to be reminded of it. Not only did the Lady note these things, but chose to let the world know to what extent she cared for it by making the "Terre du Coin (corner field)" incident an integral part of her message. Her concern was particular and personal enough to focus on three of France's complete unknowns – Melanie and Maximin and his father – and make their anxieties her own.

Her concern went beyond the village to hemispheres and continents. *"You will make this known to all my people,"* said the Lady. Her concern was intimate enough to notice wheat crumbling into dust in a man's hands. It was broad and comprehensive enough to take in the world.

***

Reflection Questions:

- Who taught you how to pray or was a good example to you in your younger life?
- How has the concern for needy person urged you to respond by helping them?

Prayer:

Mary, Mother of Mercy, your generous response to the forgotten incident in Maximin's life was a revelation of your loving concern for all your people.

You noticed that the father of Maximin was troubled to the heart about his inability to feed his family. And, with deep appreciation for his situation, your reached out to him by revivingthe memory of that event for Maximin. Thus you gave Maximin the opportunity to reach out to his father, thereby causing a renewal of faith in his father's life.

Assist us in being attentive to the needs of others, responding with the compassion and concern you expressed so generously at La Salette. We ask this through your Son, who lives with the Father and the Holy Spirit, one God, for ever and ever. Amen.

Invocation:

Our Lady of La Salette, Reconciler of Sinners, pray without ceasing for us who have recourse to you.

13

Mary's Expressions Of Hope For Us

Scripture: Romans 5:1-5,8:24-25,12:12,15:4,15:13 (*In Hope We Are Saved*)

Therefore, since we have been justified by faith, we have peace with God through our Lord Jesus Christ, through whom we have gained access [by faith] to this grace in which we stand, and we boast in hope of the glory of God...

Not only that, but we even boast of our afflictions, knowing that affliction produces endurance, and endurance, proven character, and proven character, hope, and hope does not disappoint, because the love of God has been poured out into our hearts through the holy Spirit that has been given to us...

For in hope we were saved. Now hope that sees for itself is not hope. For who hopes for what one sees? But if we hope for what we do not see, we wait with endurance... Rejoice in hope, endure in affliction, persevere in prayer... For whatever was written previously was written for our instruction, that by endurance and by the encouragement of the scriptures we might have hope...

May the God of hope fill you with all joy and peace in believing, so that you may abound in hope by the power of the holy Spirit.

Reflection:

La Salette is also clearly a message of hope meant to be given to all people, and given to them as individuals. Our Lady called even them

to the lofty responsibility of car-
rying the message of God himself
to the world. God and Our Lady
openly granted these two illiterate
children a complete trust. This
trust can also be given to anyone.
In fact, it is given, in other ways to
people who want to listen to the
Word of God and pass it on.

Our Lady's choice of Maximin and
Melanie, in spite of an absence in
them of the most common qualities and talents, is obviously an
encouragement to everyone to
aspire to closeness to Our Lord and
Our Lady. These children, who did
not pray, who did not attend Mass,
who had the most sketchy knowledge of religion, were shown to the
world as having the Lord's and the Virgin's special affection.

They were called to a highly sensitive and responsible mission despite
clearly lacking in all the gifts suitable to that mission. This is an unspoken message of La Salette: even we are called to a special mission
and loved individually and personally as Maximin and Melanie were.

By missioning these two children to her people, by repeating that this
message is directed to all of them, Mary at La Salette is surely point-
ing to the mutual responsibility we have to help one another on the
road to reconciliation and peace.

Human life is already laden enough with our own struggles – in
performing the good we desire and avoiding the evil we don't, with
our need to deal with the sadness of our own losses and agonies –
without having to cope with oppression from our own co-religionists.
But that is another necessity of life and it brings with it the consola-
tion of God-granted victories and unhoped for rewards. We discover

through her tears that the Body of Christ suffers everywhere and triumphs wherever two or three are gathered together in his name.

Reflection Questions:

- When has someone helped you in your need?
- When have you experienced the power of the promise of Jesus' words: "...where two or three are gathered together in my name, there am I in the midst of them" (Matthew 18:20)?

Prayer:

Mary, Mother of Hope, you inspire us by your words and actions at La Salette. You encourage us to learn from you how to respond to those around us with life-giving assistance to our fellow believers and those far beyond the confines of the Church.

In our experience of your presence and words to the two children at La Salette, we truly appreciate the truth of Jesus' saying, "where two or three are gathered in my name, there I am..."

We are ever-grateful that you have reminded us through your tears and actions on that Holy Mountain that the Body of Christ suffers everywhere and triumphs in hope wherever two or three are gathered together in his name. We ask this through your Son, who lives with the Father and the Holy Spirit, one God, for ever and ever. **Amen.**

Invocation:

Our Lady of La Salette, Reconciler of Sinners, pray without ceasing for us who have recourse to you.

14

Mary's Relationship With Maximin And Melanie

Scripture: 1 Corinthians 1:26-31 (*Whoever Boasts, Should Boast In The Lord*)

Consider your own calling. Not many of you were wise by human standards, not many were powerful, not many were of noble birth. Rather, God chose the foolish of the world to shame the wise, and God chose the weak of the world to shame the strong, and God chose the lowly and despised of the world, those who count for nothing, to reduce to nothing those who are something, so that no human being might boast before God. It is due to him that you are in Christ Jesus, who became for us wisdom from God, as well as righteousness, sanctification, and redemption, so that, as it is written, "Whoever boasts, should boast in the Lord."

Reflection:

There is much to learn, I believe, from the behavior of Our Lady of La Salette toward Maximin and Melanie. First, she chose them – humble, ignorant and poor. There is nothing much to envy in them. Second, they were not saints in the sense of official recognition as such by the Church. Nor will they ever be. Third, their lives after the apparition and after the local Bishop and assumed responsibility for spreading the news of La Salette, were still very ordinary. "God chose the foolish of the world to shame the wise" (1 Cor 1:27).

True, they were very often recognized as celebrities of a sort, but they manifested all the shortcomings of ordinary human beings. It would seem that Our Lady wanted to hold them up to the world as people able to serve God and the Church even though their lives gave no evidence of outstanding holiness.

It is clear that Our Lady showed them special affection and consideration throughout the apparition. The first sign of this consideration is her calling them to this special mission to the whole world. La Salette is the strong affirmation given to the people of God of the importance of their role as individuals.

Her message to all this people is clear. It is possible to be called to an important mission even if one does not have what is normally essential for this mission. God calls the ungifted, the unloved, to his own gifts and to his own love. Clearly, Our Lady of La Salette called the children to a special kind of relationship with her.

The discourse may have lasted no more than a half hour but the children's friendship with her was born on that mountain and it lasted throughout their own lifetimes

Reflection Questions:

- How do you identify with Maximin or Melanie in their situation at La Salette or in their mission of making Mary's message known?
- How has God blessed you in your life?

Prayer:

Mary, Handmaid of the Lord, your vocation from the angel to be the Mother of God was a momentous invitation but you accepted it, humbly trusting that God would help you in every way to fulfill what God asked of you.

Your example of holy simplicity and total trust in God are a shining example to us of the attitude Jesus wishes from each of us. God promises that he will use our faith, our talents, and our very person to accomplish what God wants us to do in his name.

We also ask that you stand near us as we make our way back to the Father, having done what we could to make your message known. We ask this through your Son, who lives with the Father and the Holy Spirit, one God, for ever and ever. **Amen**.

Invocation:

Our Lady of La Salette, Reconciler of Sinners, pray without ceasing for us who have recourse to you.

15

Mary Sees Christ's People Also As Her Own People

Scripture: Baruch 2:28-31b-35 (*They Shall Be My People*)

Thus you spoke through your servant Moses, the day you ordered him to write down your law in the presence of the Israelites: ...in the land of their exile they shall have a change of heart; they shall know that I, the Lord, am their God. I will give them a heart and ears that listen; and they shall praise me in the land of their exile, and shall remember my name. Then they shall turn back from their stiff-necked stubbornness, and from their evil deeds, because they shall remember the ways of their ancestors, who sinned against the Lord. And I will bring them back to the land I promised on oath to their ancestors, to Abraham, Isaac, and Jacob; and they shall rule it. I will make them increase; they shall not be few. And I will establish for them an eternal covenant: I will be their God, and they shall be my people; and I will never again remove my people Israel from the land I gave them.

Reflection:

There is a tremendous truth here. We are obliged to have Christ as the center of our existence. But if we examine the New Testament we note how we, God's creatures, have become the "center" of his life. For us he was born, lived, suffered and gave his life. For us he rose to a new life, a life he gave us as our own. Could this be the truth buried deep within the fiber of the gospel, that we can only have him as the center of our lives if we follow him in his total concern for all his people?

At La Salette, the Beautiful Lady was concerned with food and crops, but she was above all concerned with people. When she said, "my people", she meant all those persons for whom her Son died. She often referred to "my Son" as if to show the world that he was and is indeed, the center of her life. In fact, during Vatican II, Pope Paul VI proclaimed Mary the *Mother of the Church*, a title first used by St. Ambrose of Milan in the fourth century. She is our Mother and we are indeed "her people."

Reflection Questions:

•How have your parents, family or friends helped you to experience God's love through their own love for you?

•How have you experienced God's love through your local parish community or your own involvement in various ministries within and outside of the Church?

Prayer:

Mary, Mother of the Church, hear our prayer for your pilgrim people, filled with hope but still challenged in many ways as we persevere in faith. You have unearthed on that Holy Mountain that truth buried deep within the fiber of the gospel, that your Son, Jesus, must be the true center of our life.

As Mother of the Church, continue to inspire in us the desire to appreciate fully the life, death and resurrection of your Son, the supreme gift of love for his people. Help us appreciate that his same concern for all his people is expressed again by your words and efforts at reconciliation during your visit at La Salette.

Through your shining example, may your Son make of us each day a better reflection of his love. We ask this through your Son, who lives with the Father and the Holy Spirit, one God, for ever and ever. **Amen.**

Invocation:

Our Lady of La Salette, Reconciler of Sinners, pray without ceasing for us who have recourse to you.

16

Mary Sees Her Son, Jesus, As The Center Of Our Faith

Scripture: John 3:30-35 (*The Witness Of John The Baptist*)

So (the disciples of John)... said to him, "Rabbi, the one who was with you across the Jordan, to whom you testified, here he is baptizing and everyone is coming to him." John answered and said, "No one can receive anything except what has been given him from heaven. You yourselves can testify that I said [that] I am not the Messiah, but that I was sent before him. The one who has the bride is the bridegroom; the best man, who stands and listens to him, rejoices greatly at the bridegroom's voice. So this joy of mine has been made complete. He must increase; I must decrease."

Reflection:

The Lady clearly places her Son as the center of faith: she never mentions the name of Jesus but refers to him as "my Son". She evidently wants to highlight her title of "Mother of the Lord". At La Salette she appears to the world under no prerogative other than that of the Mother of God. By placing him above all else, she is telling the world that the people of God should also have Christ as its center. This is

44

not lost on the La Salette person who strives to live the spirit that the Lady wished to convey at La Salette. The apparition is heavily Christ-centered.

She wept because all the ills she noted were sins of alienation and affected God himself. Her frequent mention of "my Son", of his Name, his day, his will, the cross on her breast, prayer to him, the Mass – these are all elements and notions relating to the Godhead. La Salette is essentially concerned with the first three commandments – those that consider God alone: his name, his day, and submission and honor to him and to him alone.

Our one sin is that we are not requiting God's love. Léon Bloy said it well: "Our only misfortune is that we are not saints." The immediate consequence is the worse imaginable: abandonment by God. As Mary reminds us, *"If I want my Son not to abandon you, I am obliged to plead with him constantly...."* This penalty takes in all others and is the most frightening one God can inflict. Indeed, if God's presence is the most beautiful and loving and joy-giving of all of his gifts, abandonment by him is the height of punishment and the source of all sorrow.

The Beautiful Lady's tears are a call to return to the love and the joy that that God wanted from of old. They proclaim God's yearning for his people. When the Lady says, "my people" she is echoing the Lord's eternal longing for his own. The life of one who wholly embraces the message of La Salette should reflect that truth. As St. Paul reminds us: *For to me life is Christ* (Philippians 1:21).

Reflection Questions:

• What event in your life has helped you to experience that "as a believing family, we are all in this together" or in Paul's words, "you are the Body of Christ"?

• Who for you is an enduring example of a person who believes that "Christ must increase; I must decrease"?

Prayer:

Mary, Holy Mother of God, your apparition on the Holy Mountain of La Salette was a signature sign of God's love for his people. Your message includes references to the first three commandments given to God's people.

Your frequent mention of your Son – our praying to him, respect for his Name, his day, and the importance of the Mass, as well as the crucifix you wore – are all reminders of the fact that faith is central to who we are as your people.

May your pilgrim people always keep in our minds and hearts the words of St. Paul: "For us, life is Christ." We ask this through your Son, who lives with the Father and the Holy Spirit, one God, for ever and ever. **Amen.**

Invocation:

Our Lady of La Salette, Reconciler of Sinners, pray without ceasing for us who have recourse to you.

17

Mary's Appreciation Of The Practice Of Penance

Scripture: Luke 24:44-48 (*Jesus' Appearance To The Disciples In Jerusalem*)

Jesus said to them, "These are my words that I spoke to you while I was still with you, that everything written about me in the law of Moses and in the prophets and psalms must be fulfilled." Then he opened their minds to understand the scriptures. And he said to them, "Thus it is written that the Messiah would suffer and rise from the dead on the third day and that repentance, for the forgiveness of sins, would be preached in his name to all the nations, beginning from Jerusalem. You are witnesses of these things.

Reflection:

One of the salient facts in the story of La Salette is almost too evident for words: Our Lady did "appear". She took the initiative of coming to earth to be seen weeping and caring, to be heard saying what God himself had on his mind. She told the children to make this apparition "known to all." Reconciliation may be impossible to people alone, but God also chose to make it impossible without them. He wants reconciliation to have ministers and he wants these "ambassadors" to be joyful.

All the failings Our Lady mentioned at La Salette caused her to weep. Are we to conclude that – by conscientiously celebrating the Eucharist, honoring the Day and the Name of the Lord, restoring a life of penance and daily prayer – all of these would bring happiness and joy? All of these are, each in their own way, "other-oriented". This other is Christ himself...

The Lady insisted on penance in a powerful way, in words one would not readily expect from the Queen of Heaven. *"They go to the butcher shop like dogs,"* she said with the harsh voice of a prophet. There is no doubt remaining about the importance, the crucial nature of this command. She is saying clearly that penance is a priority of Christian existence, that without penance one cannot be a disciple. She herself says: *"How long I have suffered for you!... you will never be able to make up to me what I have endured in your behalf."* The Beautiful Lady emphasized the Lenten practice of penance as a habit of faith for her people.

Reflection Questions:

- How do you see yourself as a reconciler in your family, parish community, neighborhood or city?
- What does Lent mean to you – to give up something or do something special or both?

Prayer:

Mary, Reconciler of Sinners, you ask us to follow the ways and message of your Son. St. Paul reminds us that your Son wants us to be ministers of reconciliation and joyful "ambassadors" for all to see.

Your words – encouraging us to celebrate the Eucharist, honoring the Day and Name of your Son, and live a life of penance and daily prayer – give us the way to follow as disciples of Jesus.

With your intercession and the grace of your Son, may penance become a priority for our daily living, a habit of our faith. We ask this through your Son, who lives with the Father and the Holy Spirit, one God, for ever and ever. **Amen.**

Invocation:

Our Lady of La Salette, Reconciler of Sinners, pray without ceasing for us who have recourse to you.

<h1 style="text-align:center">18</h1>

Mary's Love Of Prayer

Scripture: Matthew 6:9-13 (*The Lord's Prayer*)

Jesus said to his disciples: This is how you are to pray: Our Father in heaven, hallowed be your name, your kingdom come, your will be done, on earth as in heaven. Give us today our daily bread; and forgive us our debts, as we forgive our debtors; and do not subject us to the final test, but deliver us from the evil one.

Reflection:

Mary said: *"You must pray, my children, morning and evening."* And she asked: *"Do you say your prayers well, my children? Ah, my children, it is very important to do so, at night and in the morning. When you don't have time, at least say an Our Father and a Hail Mary, and when you can, say more."*

"God may be of no concern to (humans), but (humanity) is of much concern to God," says Rabbi Abraham Joshua Heschel in his splendid book, Quest for God. "The only way to discover this is the ultimate way, the way of worship. For worship is a way of living, a way of seeing the world in the light of God. To worship is to rise to a higher level of existence, to see the world from the point of view of God. In worship," continues Heschel, "we discover that the ultimate way is not to have a symbol but to be a symbol, to stand for the divine" (Abraham Heschel, Quest for God, p. xii).

Abraham Heschel concludes by saying: "God is of no importance unless He is of supreme importance. Religion is not expediency. Of all the things we do, prayer is the least expedient, the least worldly, the least practical. That is why prayer is an act of self-purification." In spite of the heavy stress she laid on prayer throughout her apparition, the Lady did not impose an impossible burden on the children. There were no reproaches, no admonitions, only an injunction to say at least the minimum to keep in contact with her Son. Prayer is the most "impractical" act we do all day. It repairs nothing, builds nothing, maintains nothing, provides no human food or drink. Yet it is the vital link between God and all of these things because they should all be done for the glory of God.

The message of La Salette reminds us of the law of Sunday rest and praise, of Sunday Mass, of Lenten fast, of the honor due the name of Christ. In the world's eyes, these are all *impractical* acts... Yet all of them are considered vital to Christian life. So important are they, in fact, that if they are not accomplished, drought, famine and death will ensue. God is so pleased by his people's attitude and habits of prayers and praise that he lavishes overwhelming gifts on those who possess them.

Reflection Questions:

- What kind of prayer is most refreshing or uplifting for you?
- What various habits of prayer – different time or kinds of prayer – have you developed over your lifetime?

Prayer:

Mary, Mother of the Savior, your example of humble listening to the call of God through the angel to be the Mother of the Word of God is a singular gift to us, your pilgrim people.

In the midst of your words on the Holy Mountain – your initial warnings, and your gentle guidance to these two simple children – you did not choose to impose an impossible burden on them. You requested that their very basic lives be surrounded with brief moments of prayer and that your special mission for them be simply completed, supported by your prayers and the grace of your Son.

Lead us, in our sometimes-cluttered lives, to keep your simple goals always before us, confident that you will help us accomplish them with simplicity, faith and hope. We ask this through your Son, who lives with the Father and the Holy Spirit, one God, for ever and ever. **Amen.**

Invocation:

Our Lady of La Salette, Reconciler of Sinners, pray without ceasing for us who have recourse to you.

19

Mary Chose Maximin And Melanie, Simple Laity, To Make Her Message Known

Scripture: Ephesians 1:3-6,11-12 (*Fulfillment Through Christ*)

Blessed be the God and Father of our Lord Jesus Christ, who has blessed us in Christ with every spiritual blessing in the heavens, as he chose us in him, before the foundation of the world, to be holy and without blemish before him. In love he destined us for adoption to himself through Jesus Christ, in accord with the favor of his will, for the praise of the glory of his grace that he granted us in the beloved...

In him we were also chosen, destined in accord with the purpose of the One who accomplishes all things according to the intention of his will, so that we might exist for the praise of his glory, we who first hoped in Christ.

Reflection:

Maximin and Mélanie were laypeople. The farm of Coin episode dealt with laypeople. At the end of her visit, the Lady said, *"You will make this known to all my people"*, that is, the whole world, with no mention of the hierarchy of the Church

The strongest and most profound basis for the emergence of layperson lies less in socialfactors than in the Gospel call to follow Christ. The pursuit of spiritual perfection is no longer the exclusive domain of the religious or the priest but the duty of everyone, – not just the privilege, but the duty – originating in the Baptism of all people in the Church.

Clearly, Christ was addressing the crowds in the Sermon on the Mount from the gospel of Matthew. "When he saw the crowds, he went up the mountain, and after he had sat down, his disciples came to him. He began to teach them, saying...." (Matthew 5:1-2). In the same Sermon Christ, addressing the same people, said: "You have heard that it was said, 'You shall love your neighbor and hate your enemy.' But I say to you, love your enemies, and pray for those who persecute you, that you may be children of your heavenly Father... For if you love those who love you, what recompense will you have?... So be perfect, just as your heavenly Father is perfect (Matthew 5:43-46,48)."

The presence of the crowds makes it plain that the ideal of Christian perfection as described and commanded in the Gospel of Matthew belongs to everyone.

Our Lady of La Salette appeared to two peasant children – working children, "lay children," children of the people. Her discourse was a message to her people. *"You will make this known to all my people,"* she said and repeated to Maximin and Melanie. Nowhere in her discourse is there any allusion to clergy or hierarchy. During her assumption she turned in the direction of Rome, but this was a symbolic gesture and she did not include it in her discourse.

This same discourse was a clear appeal to the perfection of the Christian life addressed to lay people. There was a call to the Eucharist, to prayer, penance, conversion and to suffering. In addition she gave a call to honor the name of Jesus and a call to the observance of Sunday as a day to be offered to God (Fr. Silvain-Marie Giraud, M.S., Exercises Spirituels (Spiritual Exercises), pp. 294-345).

The concerns she addressed in her discourse were laypeople's concerns: the harvest; decaying wheat, rotting nuts and raisins. She jogged Maximin's memory relative to a long-forgotten conversation with his father at the farm of Coin. This father and son conversation was a layperson's dialogue. Maximin reminded his discontented father that the Lady had spoken of him in her discourse. The next day, Mr. Giraud was healed of a sickness and returned to the practice of religion.

The Beautiful Lady excludes no one from the concern of her tears and her suffering. She is speaking to all her people. But an overview of the La Salette event quickly establishes it as strongly directed toward the laity in particular.

Reflection Questions:

- What is your favorite part of the La Salette event or message?
- What place does the La Salette apparition have in your life of faith? In what ways has it taught you, changed you, or graced you?

Prayer:

Mary, Mother of God's People, hear our prayers, as we ask for your intercession for our needs and for those whom we lift up in prayer for your heavenly assistance.

As we choose to live the way and message of your Son, as echoed in your visit to La Salette, we gratefully embrace our baptismal commitment which centers us on our main purpose in life – to faithfully follow your Son each day by his grace.

Continue to give us your wisdom and guidance to keep on the "narrow path" laid out for us by your Son, that way may become a better likeness of him, who lives with the Father and the Holy Spirit, one God, for ever and ever. **Amen**.

Invocation:

Our Lady of La Salette, Reconciler of Sinners, pray without ceasing for us who have recourse to you.

20

In Mary's Apparition At La Salette, We Notice An Unseen Message

Scripture: John 19: 25-27 (*Mary becomes Mother of the Church*)

Standing by the cross of Jesus were his mother and his mother's sister, Mary the wife of Clopas, and Mary of Magdala. When Jesus saw his mother and the disciple there whom he loved, he said to his mother, "Woman, behold, your son." Then he said to the disciple, "Behold, your mother." And from that hour the disciple took her into his home.

Reflection:

Besides her words and presence at La Salette there are many elements of her unspoken message at La Salette. These include the symbols or other indications – such as her expressions, her garments, surroundings, etc. – which may indicate more about the gracious Mother of God who deigned to visit us in her merciful apparition at La Salette.

Mary appeared on a mountain, a secluded place. The stunning beauty of her surroundings still transfix pilgrims on the Holy Mountain.

Nature breathes the presence, closeness and intimacy of God. Its vast space envelopes the visitors and inspires them.

Her loving attitude of service is most evident, in that she wears a long apron by the local townspeople, perhaps typifying her attitude as a servant or handmaid of the Lord. She is free enough to serve her people without feeling put upon and adopting the view that she is not only suffering for her people but also with them as well.

Her willingness to adapt to people's needs in shown in her speech, her subject matter. When the children indicated by their facial expressions that they had difficulty understanding her, she began to speak their local patois, helping them feel more at home with her. She met the two children where they were – spiritually, mentally, and physically.

The brilliant crucifix on her breast, bearing what they described later as the live body of the Risen Lord, occupied a central place in her life and her presence at La Salette. The proposed meaning of the hammer and pincers also stressed our relationship with her Son: that is, the hammer perhaps indicating our sins which insert the nails into the hands of Jesus, and the pincers indicating our good actions which mercifully remove the nails from his hands.

Mary at La Salette bears many opposing signs. She remains the Queen of Heaven, indicated by her diadem, the bright crown of light surrounding her head yet she wears a simple peasant apron. Also as the globe of light surrounds her, she constantly weeps a Mother's tears. Around her neck the Beautiful Lady wears chains – perhaps a symbol of the burden of the sins of her people, borne for love of us. Yet we also notice the varied-colored roses around her shoulders and her feet, perhaps a reference to her plea to pray daily or the prayer-beads of the rosary. The word, "rosary" comes from the Latin, "rosari-um", meaning a crown or garland of roses.

Mary's words and actions concerning faith, prayer, penance, Eucharist and reconciliation with her Son can only be rooted in the kerygma (or basic proclamation of the gospel message) replete in the gospels. She came, she spoke, and she evangelized her children and gave them a mission – to make her message known to all her people.

These and many other elements of her merciful Apparition at La Salette can be seen as Mary's unspoken message at La Salette, urging us to follow the life and way of her Son, Jesus. She is, as John the Evangelist quotes Jesus saying: *"Behold, your mother."*

Reflection Questions:

- What would you surmise is the meaning of the hammer and pincers on the crucifix on Mary's breast?
- What might the other elements of the apparition suggest for you – the secluded place, her attitude of service, her willingness to adapt to people's needs, her crucifix, her wearing garments of the region, etc.?

Prayer:

Holy Mary, Full of Grace, at the foot of the cross in Jerusalem, on Calvary's height, you became the Mother of the Church, with the words of your Son, "Behold, your mother."

Beyond your words and actions in France, on the other Holy Mountain – your attitude of welcome and compassion, the globe of light, the crucifix, your garments, your surroundings – all these brought other unexpressed messages that we also hold dear. They encourage us to follow your lead in welcoming and meeting your people, sensing the presence of God between us, noticing that we are all equal in God's sight, and humble servants of the Lord.

Your tears at La Salette also remind us of all that your suffered for love of your Son and of his people. Be for us always a teacher in the ways of your Son. We ask this through your Son, who lives with the Father and the Holy Spirit, one God, for ever and ever. **Amen.**

Invocation:

Our Lady of La Salette, Reconciler of Sinners, pray without ceasing for us who have recourse to you.

La Salette Prayers:

Memorare to Our Lady of La Salette

Remember, Our Lady of La Salette, true Mother of Sorrows, the tears you shed for us on Calvary.

Remember also the care you have taken to keep us faithful to Christ, your Son. Having done so much for your children, you will not now abandon us.

Comforted by this consoling thought, we come to you pleading,
despite our infidelities and ingratitude.

Virgin of Reconciliation, do not reject our prayers, but intercede for us, obtain for us the grace to love Jesus above all else.

May we console you by a holy life and so come to share the eternal life Christ gained by his cross. Amen.

Invocation:

Our Lady of La Salette, Reconciler of Sinners, pray without ceasing for us who have recourse to you.

Dedication to Our Lady of La Salette

Most holy Mother, Our Lady of La Salette, who for love of me shed such bitter tears in your merciful apparition, look down with kindness upon me, as I dedicate myself to you without reserve. From this day, my glory shall be to know that I am your child. May I so live as to dry your tears and console your afflicted heart.

Beloved Mother, to you and to your blessed charge and sacred keeping and into the bosom of your mercy, for this day and for every day, and for the hour of my death I commend myself, body and soul, every hope and every joy, every trouble and every sorrow, my life and my life's end.

O dearest Mother, enlighten my understanding, direct my steps, console me by your maternal protection, so that exempt from all error, sheltered from every danger of sin, I may, with ardor and invincible courage, walk in the paths traced out for me by you and your Son. Amen.

Invocation to Our Lady of La Salette

Our Lady of La Salette, Reconciler of Sinners, Pray without ceasing for us who have recourse to you.

www.ingramcontent.com/pod-product-compliance
Lightning Source LLC
Chambersburg PA
CBHW071428040426
42445CB00012BA/1305